KEN ROBBINS

Water

THE ELEMENTS

HENRY HOLT AND COMPANY · NEW YORK

Everything that's icy, moist, or wet, from the ocean
to a drop of sweat: rivers, ponds, and streams and lakes,
raindrops, clouds and pure white snow and pounding surf,
and waterfalls and floods and tides—
this is just a partial list of all the things that water is.

CLOUDS OVER THE BRAZOS CLIFFS, LOS OJOS, NEW MEXICO

CLOUDS

All over the earth water cycles around, always going up in the air and coming back down. At the surface of all the world's oceans, streams, snow fields and lakes, water changes form: it evaporates and becomes a gas you cannot see. As water vapor, it rises high in the air, then changes back to tiny drops of liquid. It's these tiny drops, when they're drawn together, that make the clouds and affect the weather. The clouds may drift around for days, fluffy white or leaden gray, taking many different shapes, but sooner or later, there's snow or rain, and the water cycles back down to the earth again.

CLOUDS AT COOPER LAKE, NEAR WOODSTOCK, NEW YORK

CLOUDS

MORNING FOG AT YACHATS, OREGON

FOG

FOG AT THE BEACH, NANTUCKET, MASSACHUSETTS

Fog is just a cloud so low to the ground that it seems to have fallen
down from the sky. From the outside it looks like a ball of cotton.
Inside, everything is damp and looks so washed out it's as if the
whole world were fading away.

FOG

RAINSTORM OVER THE JEMEZ MOUNTAINS, SANTA FE, NEW MEXICO

R A I N

RAINSTORM, SAG HARBOR, NEW YORK

When moisture builds up in clouds, it turns them dark and gray. Tiny droplets of water collide and combine until they're too heavy to stay in the sky. They fall and we get rain. There are lots of different kinds of rain: from gentle drizzles that are barely a mist, to great downpours and violent storms. Sometimes if you go out on a beautiful day, you can see that it's raining just a mile away.

RAIN

HOH RAIN FOREST, OLYMPIC NATIONAL PARK, WASHINGTON

It's rain that makes rain forests green. They don't occur only in the tropic zone, though most of them are there. The enormous trees with their canopies of leaves, with their branches hung with moss, and masses of ferns wherever you turn—all that happens because of the rain.

RAIN FOREST

MONUMENT VALLEY, NEW MEXICO

Unlike the forest, the desert is dry, and its colors are earthy and brown. There aren't as many things living there—it's mostly rocks and barren ground. Without the usual covering of grass or shrubs or trees, we get to see how beautiful the earth itself can be.

DESERT

SLEDDING AT QUAIL HILL, AMAGANSETT, NEW YORK

SNOW

SNOW-COVERED FIELDS, LAKEVILLE, CONNECTICUT

Snow falls when cold air has crystallized the rain. Raindrops become snowflakes. No two flakes are ever the same. When snow piles up, it covers the earth in a blanket of white, turning hills into bobsled runs and changing everything in sight.

SNOW

FROZEN POND, EAST HAMPTON, NEW YORK

ICE

When water gets cold enough, it's not a liquid anymore—it's no longer wet, and the stuff won't pour. It's cold and hard and it feels almost dry. In winter a pond or a lake may freeze (or the surface of it does, at least). If the ice is thick enough, you can put on your skates and glide on the frozen water.

ICE CUBES AND GLASS

GLACIERS, FROM HURRICANE RIDGE, OLYMPIC NATIONAL PARK, WASHINGTON

GLACIER

High in the mountains it stays so cold that the snow never completely goes away, even in summer. When the snow piles up and packs down year after year, it's called a glacier. Glaciers flow like rivers do, but so slowly you can't see them move: perhaps a tenth of an inch a day. That's enough in several thousand years to hollow out a valley or level a hill.

PUDDLE, EAST HAMPTON, NEW YORK

When rain falls, most of it soaks right into the ground, but some collects in puddles and stays around for a while before it disappears. Tiny creatures that you can't even see live their whole short lives in puddles that dry up in just a few days.

PUDDLES, PONDS

CATTLE POND NEAR RED CLOUD, NEBRASKA

Ponds last longer than puddles do, but once in a while they dry up too. They give a home to living things like snails, small fishes, frogs and slugs, water plants and birds and bugs.

GREAT BLUE HERON, EAST HAMPTON, NEW YORK

LAKES

COOPER LAKE, NEAR WOODSTOCK, NEW YORK

A lake is a body of water bigger than a pond. Fish live in most lakes, waterfowl live on them. Many sorts of animals live on or in or by them. Some lakes are large and some are small, some are shallow, some are deep, some are fresh, some are salty like the sea. Some are used as reservoirs for the water people need. Some are pristine, undisturbed, in the peaceful wilderness, some are overused by people and have become polluted messes.

LAKES

MOLTNOMA FALLS, COLUMBIA GORGE, OREGON

WATERFALLS

Water runs in brooks and streams, rills and rivulets, branches and creeks, restlessly flowing, and always downhill. When the downhill slope is very steep, water runs madly in a frothing, plunging, white-water heap. And if there is a cliff in its path—it leaps without a moment's pause and becomes a beautiful, roaring waterfall.

MOUNTAIN STREAM, NEAR BONDVILLE, NEW HAMPSHIRE

WATERFALLS

RIO GRANDE, NEAR TAOS, NEW MEXICO

RIVERS

CHAMA RIVER, ABIQUIU, NEW MEXICO

Brooks flow into streams and streams into rivers, moving downhill with amazing power, scouring their banks, hour by hour, year after year. Slowly but surely water carves up the land, picking up salt and silt and sand as it goes, gouging out a gorge that can be a mile deep. When the river levels off and loses speed, some of that salt and silt and sand get left behind to build up the land.

RIVERS

PACIFIC COAST, HECETA LIGHTHOUSE, NEAR YACHATS, OREGON

O C E A N S

ATLANTIC COAST, NAPEAGUE BEACH, AMAGANSETT, NEW YORK

At the edge of the vast mysterious sea, people come to the beach to play and swim. Sailors skim over the surface of the sea, without knowing much about what's underneath. Divers may dive down a few hundred feet, but parts of the ocean are seven miles deep. People have never been to most places on the ocean floor, and there are creatures there that no one's seen. Some ancient sea is probably where life first arose three thousand million years ago.

OCEANS

THOUSAND SPRINGS AREA, NEAR HAGERMAN, IDAHO

It's true that water tends to run to the sea. But not all rain and melted snow go directly to the ocean. If it hasn't been drunk by living things, or used by heavy industry, or frozen solid in a block of ice; if it's not trapped in a pond or lake; if it hasn't become part of a river or stream, then it probably sinks into the earth. And as it seeps down, it's filtered and cleaned. Underground, it may stay for years, trapped in layers of gravel and rock, but sometimes it finds its way back up. That's a wonderful thing, a gift of clean water from the earth to us: it's called a spring.

SPRINGS

In certain places, water surfaces in a most unusual, spectacular way. Deep in the earth it's hot enough to melt a rock. When underground water meets that heat, the water begins to expand and boil. And if there happens to be a crack in the earth to let the water escape, then water and steam shoot up in the air with a hiss and a roar, and that is what's called a geyser in play.

OLD FAITHFUL GEYSER,
YELLOWSTONE NATIONAL PARK, WYOMING

WATER WELL,
LITCHFIELD, CONNECTICUT

WELL PUMP, AMAGANSETT, NEW YORK

Most of the water that collects underground, left on its own, would never rise. So people dig wells in the earth to get to where that water lies. The well might be just ten feet deep or it might be a hundred and fifty. You can never quite tell when you're digging a well just when you're going to hit water.

Every living thing has to have water to survive. Every plant or animal, bird or bug, germ or virus, maple tree or farmer's daughter—every one of them needs water. Your body is made mostly of water, but you lose some when you pee or sweat. You get some back when you eat your food, because food is largely water too. But the best way to get the water you need is to quench your thirst by taking a drink.

RUNNER, TEN KILOMETER RACE, EAST HAMPTON, NEW YORK

IRRIGATED FIELDS NEAR RED CLOUD, NEBRASKA

Crops that are grown on a farmer's land have to have enough rain or they'll die. If it doesn't rain, the farmer only has one choice: he's got to bring water from some other source. He can get that water by draining a lake, diverting a river, or pumping a well. It's called irrigation, and it's a key to growing more crops than there would otherwise be.

IRRIGATION

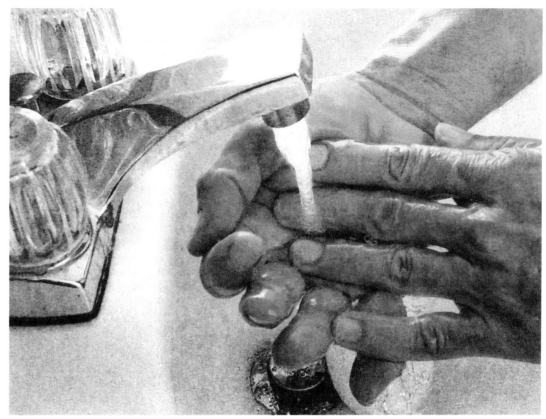

WASHING HANDS

Flowing water will wash dirt away, which makes it useful for getting things clean—dirty dishes and laundry and windows, and most especially you and me. Think about the water that comes from your tap. You use it to wash your hands, your dishes and laundry, maybe your food. It flushes the waste from your toilet bowl, too. Every town and city has sewers to carry the waste water away. But the next time you wash something, ask yourself this: where in the world does the waste water go?

WASHING

GLEN CANYON DAM, PAGE, ARIZONA

DAMS

BEAVER DAM, NEW HAMPSHIRE

Building a dam can hold back a river, creating electrical power and making a lake where dry land was before. The lake may be used for swimming and boating, the water for irrigation or drinking. But who decided to build that dam and what were they thinking when they kept that river from running to the sea? What if I think that water belongs to me? And what about the places farther downstream? Everything changes when a dam is built, and often in ways that can't be foreseen. A dam is a complicated thing.

DAMS

FLOODED STREET, BONAPARTE, IOWA

FLOODS

HURRICANE FLOODING, EAST HAMPTON, NEW YORK

When rivers follow their usual course, and ocean waves break on the shore where they belong, then things are just as they should be. But too much rain or a storm at sea can be a great catastrophe. Gigantic tides can wipe out beaches, sweeping everything aside. Swollen rivers leap their banks, and water flows down city streets, homes are ruined, fields are flooded, sometimes people's lives are lost. Floods will happen—they're only natural, and they often do no harm at all. But sometimes when they happen there's an awful human cost.

FLOODS

BAYMEN, ACCABONAC HARBOR, EAST HAMPTON, NEW YORK

B O A T S

SAILBOATS, FRENCHMAN'S BAY, BAR HARBOR, MAINE

There's another way in which water is useful. It makes a road on which boats can float, toting loads of goods and people from one place to another. Riverboats and ocean liners, ferries, barges, and canoes—boats of every size and shape float on rivers, ponds and oceans, straits and channels, bays and lakes.

FISHING, THREE MILE HARBOR, EAST HAMPTON, NEW YORK

F I S H I N G

SURF CASTERS, EAST HAMPTON, NEW YORK

Anyone who's ever eaten tuna salad, crawfish stew, caviar or lobster meat, steamer clams, or salmon steaks, flounder, mackerel or trout, or any other seafood dish, or any other fish at all, has reason to be grateful for what the fisherman hauls up. The oceans are so large and rivers so wide that people used to think that the fish would always be there—an inexhaustible supply of food. But fish are just like anything else, like any part of the world's wealth: if we take too much, it won't be there when we need it.

FISHING

STEAM ENGINE, NEW HOPE, PENNSYLVANIA

POWER

WATERWHEEL, BUCKS COUNTY, PENNSYLVANIA

Water is a source of power. The force of flowing water can turn a
mill for grinding grain and making flour. The power of steam can
drive a train. Even the tide's unending motion can be harnessed
to drive machines. When rushing water spins the wheels of
hydroelectric power plants, the power that plants produce can run
your computer and light your house.

POWER

SWIMMING HOLE, NEAR HAGERMON, IDAHO

POOL, EAST HAMATON, NEW YORK

Water is important in serious ways.
But it's also good on summer days
for swimming, boating, fishing,
diving, fooling, splashing, and
in general . . . cooling off.

SWIMMING

NICHOLS FOUNTAIN, KANSAS CITY, MISSOURI

Water is such a wonderful, joyful thing that just to hear the sound it makes, just to watch it dance in the light, people build fountains in public places and throw their coins in . . . just for luck.

FOUNTAINS

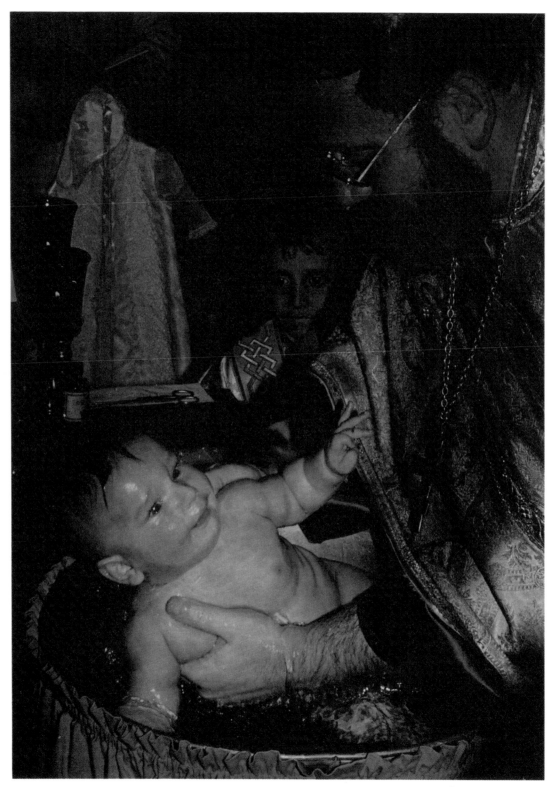

EASTERN RITE BAPTISM, NEW YORK, NEW YORK

R I T U A L

Water is one of the sacred things. In every culture and every country, people consider it holy and good. It shouldn't ever be taken for granted, wasted, or soiled needlessly. In more ways than we often realize, it's the fountain and source of life on earth.

For
Rebecca Mary Bowen Goodman

Thanks to Brenda Bowen, Faith Hamlin, John Ford, Irene Tully, and most especially
to my life's partner and most excellent traveling companion, Maria

All hand coloring by Ken Robbins
Note: The photograph on page 43 shows a breast-shot waterwheel known as Bromley's Mill
located along the Cuttalossa Creek in Bucks County, Pennsylvania.

Photo Notes and Credits
All photographs by Ken Robbins except as noted below:
Beaver Dam photograph on page 35 by N. Pecnic/Visuals Unlimited
Flood picture on page 36 by Bob Firth/Firth PhotoBank
Flood picture on page 37 by Bob Firth/Firth PhotoBank
Snowflake photo on page 48 by R. Walters/Visuals Unlimited

Henry Holt and Company, Inc. / *Publishers since 1866*
115 West 18th Street / New York, New York 10011

Henry Holt is a registered trademark of Henry Holt and Company, Inc.
Copyright © 1994 by Ken Robbins. All rights reserved.
Published in Canada by Fitzhenry & Whiteside Ltd.,
195 Allstate Parkway, Markham, Ontario L3R 4T8.

Library of Congress Cataloging-in-Publication Data
Robbins, Ken. Water / by Ken Robbins.
1. Water—Juvenile literature. [1. Water.] I. Title.
GB662.3.R63 1994 551.48—dc20 93-44632

ISBN 0-8050-2257-0

First Edition—1994

Printed in the United States of America on acid-free paper. ∞

1 3 5 7 9 10 8 6 4 2

The photographs for this book are hand colored with water-based dyes.